LAUREL BURCH QUILTS

KINDRED CREATURES

C&T PUBLISHING

Many thanks to the following companies for their generous donations of materials used in the making of the quilts.

♥ Benartex Inc.
♥ Coats & Clark
♥ Freudenberg Nonwovens, Pellon Division
♥ Hoffman California Fabrics
♥ Marcus Brothers Textiles, Inc.
♥ Northcott Silk Inc.
♥ P&B Textiles
♥ Plaid Enterprises, Inc.
♥ Robert Kaufman Company
♥ Timeless Treasures Fabrics, Inc.
♥ YLI Threads

Development Editor: Cyndy Lyle Rymer
Technical Editor: Lynn Koolish
Design Director: Aliza Shalit
Cover and Book Design & Production: Aliza Shalit
Graphic Illustrations: Aliza Shalit, AK Design
Production Assistant: Tim Manibusan
Cover Image: Detail of *Kindred Creatures*, 30½" square, Nancy Odom, 2000. Photo by Sharon Risedorph
Photos of Laurel Burch original art by Rick Sara
Set Shot Photo Styling: Aliza Shalit and Laurel Burch
Photo Assistants: Diane Pedersen and Cyndy Rymer
Set shot and how-to photography by Steve Buckley
Quilt Photo on page 77: Sharon Risedorph
Dog Photo Details pp. 57-61: Amy Marson

Attention Teachers:
C&T Publishing, Inc. encourages you to use this book as a text for teaching. Contact us at 800-284-1114 or www.ctpub.com for more information about the C&T Teachers Program.

Library of Congress Cataloging-in-Publication Data

Burch, Laurel.
    Laurel Burch quilts : kindred creatures / Laurel Burch.
        p. cm.
Includes bibliographical references and index.
    ISBN 1-57120-160-2 (paper trade)
    1. Appliqué—Patterns. 2. Quilts. 3. Burch, Laurel—Themes, motives. I. Title.
TT779 .B774 2001
746.46'041—dc21
                            2001001983

Published by C&T Publishing, Inc.
P.O. Box 1456
Lafayette, California 94549

Printed in Hong Kong
10 9 8 7 6 5 4 3 2 1

DEDICATION

It was my mother, Anne Harte, who inspired my insatiable love for fabrics, ribbons, buttons, and embellishments. And the infinite ways rainbow colors and textures could be brought together magically by a needle and thread.

From practical to playful, Mom created our clothing, bedding, and dolls. She was a quintessential seamstress extraordinaire, and my awe of every tiny French knot she tied, and little satin rosebud she made, left its indelible imprint on my heart and life as an artist.

And so it is to my mom, Anne, I lovingly dedicate this book.

And to my sisters, Suzanne and Jil.

The precious threads that bind us to this day are woven together by our shared passion to create.

A gift to us all, Mom's spirit lives on through her daughters' hands and hearts, and we thank her for her inspiration to pass this on for many generations to come.

Laurel Burch

ACKNOWLEDGMENTS

Heartfelt thanks to the many "kindred creatures" who so lovingly brought the vision for this book to fruition at C&T Publishing: Cyndy Lyle Rymer, Aliza Shalit, Lynn Koolish, Todd Hensley, Diane Pedersen, Joyce Lytle, Amy Marson, Jan Grigsby, and Peggy Kass.

To the quintessential quiltmakers who magically transformed my paintings into the magnificent quilts that are the heart of the book, and to my own "inner sanctum" support team: Jay Burch, Rick Sara, Julie Buelow, Will Schneider, Ranny Riley, and Wendy Tyler, who made this dream possible for me in so very many ways.

TABLE OF CONTENTS

WELCOME TO THE WORLD OF KINDRED CREATURES

Dear Quilting Friends,

As a child, I lived in the infinite realm of my imagination—drawing in secret jungles with mythical tigers, prancing across a desert oasis wearing tribal jewels, soaring in dreams with rainbow-colored birds to faraway places.

As I grew, so grew my passion to create, and to share. Through my art myths emerged, stories came alive, kindred spirits connected.

The purpose of my art is to inspire living from the heart. I want to create gifts that celebrate life in the most intimate and precious ways possible, for ourselves and for each other.

My paintings have become the most intimate expressions of all that is most precious to me. Who can deny that we share a connection with all living creatures? And what better way to celebrate that connection than through creating a work of art? I invite you to interpret my designs while creating quilts of your own.

It seems to be no accident that C&T and I were brought together to create this book. My mother, who was a wonderful seamstress, was a magician with needle and thread, fabrics, and ribbons, and it was her sharing of these materials with me that began my love affair with sewing.

While Mom expanded her sewing skills, I began to develop my painting more. Threads, fabrics, buttons, ribbons, and yarns definitely became part of my paintings, and this was my own way of incorporating my mother's craft into my individual style and expression. My "Artwear" dresses, made in the 1960s, were beaded, embroidered, appliquéd, painted, and collaged with everything from horsehair to Native American trade beads, and even old coins from other countries. I called them my Global Spirit dresses. I feel such a kinship with quilters, as they share the same passion for fabric and color.

Someday I hope to put down my paintbrush and pick up a needle and thread, and try my hand at doing exactly what you love to do: make paintings using fabric and thread, and beads, and buttons. I love the fact that the possibilities are endless, the materials quilters use so rich and varied.

Thank you for this wonderful opportunity to share my colorful world, and bring kindred creatures together through my art and your own.

Laurel Burch

WALKING IN LAURELAND

What a colorful journey you begin when you set foot in Laurel's world. Her use of bright, saturated color and attention to the smallest details will draw you in and unleash your creativity. Spend some time studying her original paintings as your source for inspiration; let your imagination connect with Laurel's kindred creatures. We highly recommend that you give some of the painting and other embellishing techniques a try. You'll feel as great as you did when you fingerpainted all those years ago. Interpreting one of Laurel's original paintings offers so many opportunities to stretch your creative abilities as far as you choose to go.

If you're new to quilting, check out the list of references in the back of the book for some good beginning how-to quilt books. These books will tell you everything you need to know about basic piecing, appliqué, adding borders, quilting, and binding.

Be sure to refer to pages 86-94 before you begin. All of the Tips & Techniques described will help you get started with any of these delightful projects.

Begin by taking the book to the nearest copy center and have the patterns you want to use enlarged or reduced to any size you are comfortable with. Ready-to-use pullouts are offered at the back of the book for the most detailed quilts–*Carlotta in the Secret Garden* and *Kindred Creatures*. Because of the large variety of shapes used in both of these quilts, they offer many opportunities to show off your favorite fabrics and decorative stitching.

Most of the projects follow the same basic process of selecting and cutting your fabric appliqués, embellishing if desired with paint or thread,

stitching them to a background, and finishing off by adding borders, quilting, and binding or framing. For ease of construction, most of these quilts can be machine appliquéd using fusible web. If you want to try a project but you don't sew, the *Flutter-bye Frame* on page 24 is a no-sew project. You can also apply this no-sew technique to the other projects in this book.

The true beauty of these projects is that there are so many ways to add your personal touch. Using fabric paints you can paint on details and layers of color—including metallic touches—or you can embellish with machine stitches. Satin stitching is a wonderful way to add another touch of color, and to secure the raw edges of the appliqués. Quilters who own an embroidery machine will find that these quilts are great canvases for any stitch they can create.

PATTERN NOTE: All of the black lines in the patterns indicate individual shapes that need to be cut out. The tinted lines indicate areas to be embellished with painting or stitching.

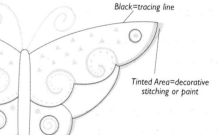

Black=tracing line

Tinted Area=decorative stitching or paint

MARIAH MOONBEAM AND FRIEND

AS AN ARTIST
MY LIFE IS DEEPLY
CONNECTED
TO THE PURPOSE
AND JOY
OF CREATING FOR
SO MANY WONDERFUL
KINDRED SPIRITS...

WE SHARE SIMILAR
PASSIONS AND DREAMS
ABOUT THE IMPORTANCE
OF MAGIC IN OUR
EVERY DAY LIVES, AND
THE KINSHIP BETWEEN
ALL LIVING THINGS
♥

Laurel

MARIAH MOONBEAM & FRIEND

Finished Quilt Size: 19" × 23"
Machine appliquéd and quilted by Cynthia Moody Wheeler, Hoover, Alabama, 2000.
Fabric generously donated by Robert Kaufman Company.

MATERIALS

♥ Yellow: ⅔ yard for background and collar base
♥ Teal: ¾ yard for outer border, ears, and nose
♥ Black: 1 yard for inner borders, backing, and binding
♥ Medium purple: ½ yard for face
♥ Scraps (no more than 6" squares) of the following: medium and dark pink, medium and dark red, orange, a variety of light and dark greens, tan, blue, dark purple
♥ Batting: 23" × 29"
♥ Fusible web: 2 yards
♥ Tear-away stabilizer: ¾ yard
♥ Threads for decorative stitching: metallic gold and black
♥ Fabric paint: gold
♥ Black Pigma fine point pen

CUTTING

Yellow:

Background: Cut one 15" × 19" rectangle (to be trimmed after appliqué).

Black:

Side inner borders: Cut two strips 1¼"-wide × 17½".
Top and bottom inner borders: Cut two strips 1¼"-wide × 15".
Backing: Cut one 23" × 29" rectangle.
Binding: Cut two strips 2¼"-wide × width of the fabric.

Teal:

Outer borders: Cut four strips 2½"-wide × 19".

TIPS FOR MAKING MARIAH MOONBEAM AND FRIEND

1. Have the pattern enlarged 210% before you begin. See instructions for machine appliqué using fusible web on page 87.

2. If you are going to paint, cover your workspace to protect it. You can either paint or appliqué the hearts and eye details onto the purple face before fusing the face

to the background. If you choose to paint the details make sure you let them dry completely before fusing Mariah's face onto the backgound.

If you machine appliqué the detail mentioned above, the decorative satin stitching should be done in two phases. First pin or baste the tear-away stabilizer to the back of the piece. In layered areas such as the eyes, satin stitch around each layer after all of the individual layers have been fused together, but before fusing to the final background. Save the satin stitching around the major pieces—such as Mariah's face and the bird—as a final step to be completed after all of the layers have been fused to the background.

3. The collar Mariah is wearing should be made as a separate layer. Yellow is used as a base for the flowers and leaves. The red flower in the center is one piece of fabric. Outline the flower petals with satin stitching in gold metallic thread. After the leaves are fused to the background, use black thread and a straight stitch to add the veins, and a fine black permanent pen to make the dots.

Fusing the fabric shapes onto the collar

4. Fuse all of the pieces in place, then lightly draw in the details on Mariah's ears and on the wings of the bird before stitching.

5. Back the piece with tear-away stabilizer, then satin stitch around all of the raw edges.

6. Trim the finished center to 13½" × 17½", keeping the design centered.

7. Add the whiskers using black thread and a narrow zigzag stitch.

8. Use the eraser end of a fat pencil and gold fabric paint to stamp the dots on the black border strips. Let dry completely.

9. Add the black inner side borders, then the top and bottom borders. Press seams toward the border.

10. Add the teal outer side borders, then the top and bottom borders. Press seams toward the borders.

11. Layer your quilt top with the batting and backing. Pin or thread baste the layers together.

12. Stitch in-the-ditch around Mariah's face, then along both edges of the black border. Quilt a diamond pattern in the teal border. Bind or finish as desired.

A fabric key can help you keep track of the fabrics you plan to use.

FLUTTER-BYE SONG

GATHER WILD HONEY
DRINK MOON BEAMS
SLEEP IN THE STARS
AND REMEMBER TO
LAUGH, TO DREAM,
TO FEEL THE COLORS
OF YOUR SHINING SOUL.
MOST of ALL,
PRETEND YOU HAVE
BUTTERFLY WINGS
AND USE THEM!

Laurel

Projects from left to right:
Folkloric Flutter-byes (page 18);
No-Sew Flutterbye Frame (top, page 24);
Summer Flutter-bye (page 16).

SUMMER FLUTTER-BYE

Finished Quilt Size: 19½" square
Hand appliquéd and machine quilted by Nancy Busby, Rio Vista, California, 2000.
Fabric generously donated by P&B Textiles.
Please note that instructions are for a small wallhanging, not a pillow.

MATERIALS

♥ Black: 1 yard for background, outer border, and backing

♥ Turquoise: ¼ yard for inner border and binding

♥ Scraps of the following for the flutter-bye:
yellow-orange, light violet, purple, fuchsia, green,
orange, gold lamé (optional)

♥ Batting: 24" square

♥ Embroidery floss (optional): silver-black, gold, metallic gold

♥ If you want to machine appliqué:
½ yard fusible web and ½ yard tear-away stabilizer

♥ Fabric paint: gold (optional, for dots if not appliquéd)

CUTTING

Black:
Background: Cut one 14" square (to be trimmed after appliqué).

Top and bottom outer borders: Cut two strips 3"-wide × 14½".

Side outer borders: Cut two strips 3"-wide × 19½".

Backing: Cut one 24" square.

Turquoise:
Top and bottom inner borders: Cut two strips 1½"-wide × 12½".

Side inner borders: Cut two strips 1½"-wide × 14½".

Binding: Cut two strips 2¼"-wide × width of fabric.

TIPS FOR MAKING SUMMER FLUTTER-BYE

1. Have the pattern enlarged 200% before you begin. If you plan to machine appliqué, see instructions for using fusible web on page 87. Begin by planning and cutting your appliqué shapes.

2. Hand or machine appliqué all of the flutter-bye shapes in place. Start by appliquéing the smaller pieces onto the larger pieces.

3. The fabric for the optional smaller outside circles is gold/black polyester-backed lamé. Fusible interfacing was used as a backing for the lamé. These can also be painted on; see the photo on page 88.

4. Chain stitch the antennae using two strands of gold embroidery thread.

5. Stem-stitch the wing spirals with one strand of metallic gold embroidery thread, or use a gold metallic fabric pen for this detail.

6. Trim the background to 12½" square, keeping the design centered.

Note: If you prefer to paint the gold dots, it's best to do so before adding the borders to your piece.

7. Add the turquoise inner top and bottom borders, then the side borders. Press seams toward the borders. Paint or fuse the gold dots in the turquoise border, then blanket-stitch the fused dots with silver/black embroidery thread using the center of the dot as the pivot point.

8. Add the black top and bottom outer borders, then the side borders. Press seams toward the borders.

9. Layer your quilt top with the batting and backing, and quilt as desired. Bind or finish as desired.

 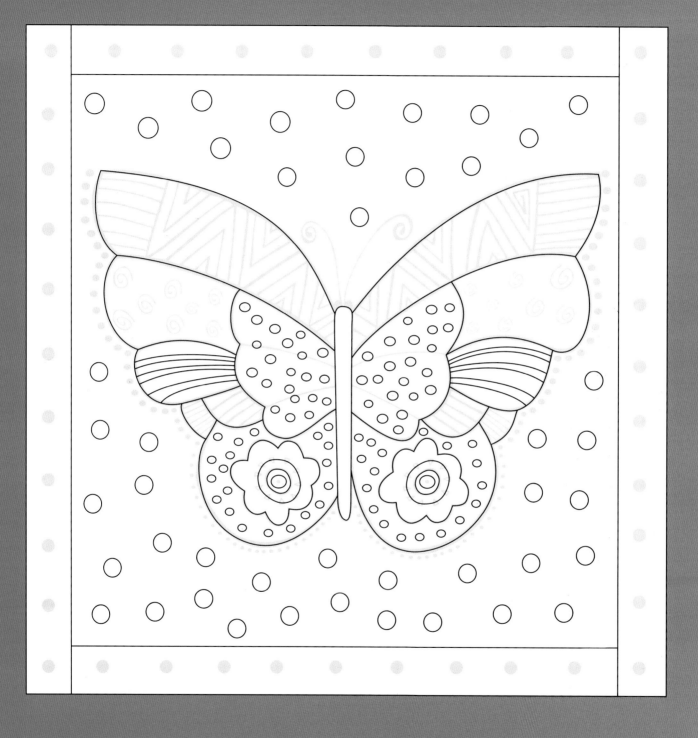

FOLKLORIC FLUTTER-BYES

Finished Quilt Size: 17" x 42"
Machine appliquéd and quilted by Cynthia Moody Wheeler, Hoover, Alabama, 2000.
Fabric generously donated by Robert Kaufman Company.

MATERIALS

♥ Black: 2 yards for borders, backing, and binding
♥ Blue, lime green, and fuchsia:
  11" squares of each for flutter-bye backgrounds
♥ Turquoise, yellow, and purple prints:
  ¼ yard of each for borders
♥ Oranges, dark blue, light blue, and yellow:
  8" squares of each for larger flutter-bye parts
♥ Scraps of the following:
  medium and dark pink, medium and dark purple,
  yellow print, light green, blue, dark magenta
♥ Batting: 21" x 46"
♥ Fusible web: 2 yards
♥ Tear-away stabilizer: 1 yard
♥ Threads for decorative stitching: metallic gold and black
♥ Fabric paint: gold, purple, orange, black, and white
♥ Stamping tools, small paintbrush
♥ Decorative beads (optional)

CUTTING

All of the background squares will be trimmed
after appliqué.

Block 1:

Background: Cut one 11" blue square.

Second inner borders: Cut two turquoise print strips
1¼"-wide x 10½" for the sides and two strips
1¼"-wide x 12" for the top and bottom borders.

Cut flutter-bye shapes in the colors of your choice.

Block 2:

Background: Cut one 11" lime green square.

Second inner borders: Cut two yellow print strips
1¼"-wide x 10½" for the sides and two strips
1¼"-wide x 12" for the top and bottom borders.

Cut flutter-bye shapes in the colors of your choice.

Block 3:

Background: Cut one 11" fuchsia square.

Second inner borders: Cut two purple print strips
1¼"-wide x 10½" for the sides and two strips
1¼"-wide x 12" for the top and bottom borders.

Cut flutter-bye shapes in the colors of your choice.

Black:

First inner borders: Cut six strips ¾"-wide x 10"
for the sides and six strips ¾"-wide x 10½" for
the top and bottom.

Sashing between blocks: Cut two strips 1½"-wide x 12".

Outer border: Cut two strips 3"-wide x 37" for the sides
and two strips 3"-wide x 17" for the top and bottom.

Backing: Cut one 21" x 46" rectangle.

Binding: Cut four strips 2¼"-wide x width of fabric.

TIPS FOR MAKING FOLKLORIC FLUTTER-BYES

1. Have the patterns enlarged 200% before you begin. See instructions for machine appliqué using fusible web on page 87.

2. To prepare the background squares, first cover your workspace to protect it, then stamp dots on the background squares using the end of an eraser on a chunky pencil and fabric paint. Let dry completely. Add white dots in the center of the stamped dots by dipping the end of a small paintbrush in white paint and then "dotting" it in the center of each of the larger stamped dots. Let paint dry completely. Remember that you don't need to paint the centers of the blocks where the background fabric will be covered by the flutter-byes.

3. Cut all flutter-bye shapes and fuse in place, then lightly draw in details that will be painted or stitched later, such as antennae and curves on wings.

18

Two colors are used to outline each shape.

4. Pin or baste the tear-away stabilizer to the back of each block. Satin stitch around all the raw edges before sewing the flutter-bye blocks together. Note that some shapes are outlined with two colors, usually along the outer edge—stitch the inner color first, then the outer color.

5. When the appliqué is complete, trim each block to 10" square, keeping the design centered.

6. Add the black inner side borders to each block, then the top and bottom borders. Press seams toward the border.

7. Add the second colored side borders to each block, then the top and bottom borders. Press seams toward the borders.

8. Sew the 1½" x 12" black sashing strips between the blocks. Press toward the sashing.

9. Add the black outer side borders, then the top and bottom borders. Press seams toward the border.

Note: Add any decorative beading *after* you have finished the quilting.

10. Layer your quilt top with the batting and backing. Pin or thread baste the layers together.

11. A suggested plan for the quilting is to stitch around each flutter-bye, the wing shapes, and the bodies. Stitch in-the-ditch along the inner edge of the narrow black border and along the outer edge of the flutter-bye borders. In the outer border, quilt two straight lines ¾" apart to divide it into thirds. Bind or finish as desired.

folkloric flutter-bye pattern 1

folkloric flutter-bye pattern 2

NO-SEW FLUTTER-BYE FRAME

Finished Frame Size: 24" square
Made by Lynn Koolish, Berkeley, CA, 2001.

MATERIALS

♥ Scraps of oranges, yellows, light and dark purples, pinks, turquoises, lime greens. Please note that scraps for the bottom layer of the flutter-byes need to be at least 5" x 10".

♥ Fusible web: 3 yards

♥ Heavy-weight fusible interfacing: 2 yards

♥ Fabric paint:
   assorted opaque colors including white and black

♥ Fabric pen: Black

♥ Small pieces of sponge

♥ Small paint brushes

♥ White cloth-wrapped wire for antennae
   (available in craft or floral supplies stores)

♥ Stamping tools, small paint brushes

♥ Clear glue

♥ Self-adhesive hook and loop fastener dots

♥ 24" square piece of mat board with
   a 10" square opening

♥ 24" square metal sectional frame (readily available at art or craft stores; most come two sections per package, so you might need to buy two packages)

TIPS FOR MAKING THE NO-SEW FLUTTER-BYE FRAME

This project is constructed a little differently than described in the general instructions because no sewing is involved.

1. Enlarge patterns 160%. Rather than tracing onto the fusible web, trace the shapes directly onto your fabric, lightly drawing details that you will be painting over. It's easiest to build up the layers of fabric starting from a base that is cut out of the entire flutter-bye shape.

Plan on adding layers from the bottom up. This is one project where it's okay to build up multiple layers of fabric.

2. After you trace the shapes, iron on pieces of fusible web that extend just beyond the lines of your drawn shapes.

3. Cover your workspace to protect it before you begin to paint or draw all the details. The swirls, triangles, dots, curliques, etc. can be drawn with permanent ink pens, painted with small brushes, or stamped with store-bought or hand-made stamps. Again, the eraser end of a pencil is perfect for making dots. Make sure one layer of paint or ink is dry before applying a second layer. The Resources on page 94 lists sources for all the materials and tools for this project.

4. Outline all of the shapes with black or white fabric paint or pen before they are cut out. (If you outline after the shapes are cut, the fabric is more likely to fray.)

5. When the paint is completely dry, cut out the shapes with sharp scissors.

6. Fuse the layers together. If you want to give the flutter-byes extra body so the wings stand away from the mat board and frame, you can add an extra layer of fabric and fusible interfacing. Cut an extra piece of fabric and a piece of fusible interfacing a little larger than the finished flutter-bye.

Fuse the interfacing to the extra piece of fabric. Then iron the fusible web to the interfaced fabric. Fuse this to the back of the flutter-bye and trim the excess fabric and interfacing.

7. Curl the ends of the wrapped wire around a pencil, then glue on for the antennae. A little clear glue on the ends of the wire will prevent fraying.

8. Arrange the flutter-byes on the mat board. To allow the flutter-byes to be removable, put two pieces of the loop side of the fastener dots on each flutter-bye body and put the corresponding hook side on the mat board.

This method also leaves the wings free, adding dimension to the frame. If you prefer, you can glue the flutter-byes directly to the mat board.

flutter-bye frame patterns

flutter-bye frame patterns

HORSE SPIRIT

Standing above the
valley of ELK Canyon
at sunset. Suddenly the
thunderous vibration
of hooves moved the

earth beneath my feet.
A vision of unforgettable
power and beauty...
Wild horses. Galloping in
separate family bands
down the dry riverbed
in front of me, toward
the meadow for the night.

MY heart pounding along with
the hooves of the horses.
a part of the indelible vision
and memory of this moment
lives within every image of
horses i will ever create.

Laurel

EMBRACING HORSES

Finished Quilt Size: 30" x 31"
Machine appliquéd and quilted by Laura and Rita DeMarco, Blairsville, Georgia, 2000.
Fabric generously donated by Benartex Inc.

MATERIALS

▼ Light gold: ⅞ yard for background
▼ Black: 2¼ yards for horses, backing, binding
▼ Blue: 1 yard for mane
▼ Red-purple: ¼ yard for mane
▼ Scraps of the following: red, orange, dark purple for mane
▼ Dark gold: ½ yard for mane and outside border
▼ Batting: 34" x 35"
▼ Fusible web: 2 yards
▼ Tear-away stabilizer: 2 yards
▼ Threads for decorative stitching: black and gold

CUTTING

Light Gold:

Background: Cut one 29" x 30" rectangle.

Dark Gold:

Top and bottom borders: Cut two strips 1½"-wide x 28".
Side borders: Cut two strips 1½"-wide x 31".

Black:

Backing: Cut one 34" x 35" rectangle.
Binding: Cut four strips 2¼"-wide x width of fabric.

TIPS FOR MAKING EMBRACING HORSES

1. Have the pattern enlarged 400% before you begin. See instructions for machine appliqué using fusible web on page 87.

2. Prepare the horse's mane first: cut and use a piece of blue as a base, and fuse the other colors to it.

3. Pin or thread baste the stabilizer to the back of the mane piece.

Using black thread, satin stitch between the "stripes" of the mane before fusing it with the other shapes onto the light gold background.

4. Cut the horses from one black piece of fabric, and fuse the eye pieces onto the black background piece. Pin or thread-baste stabilizer to the back. Use a wide satin stitch with gold thread to outline the features of the two horses. Remove stabilizer.

Detail of satin stitching

5. Layer the mane and horses onto the background. Back with stabilizer and satin stitch around the outside of the mane.

6. Trim quilt top to 28" x 29", keeping the *Embracing Horses* design centered.

7. Add the dark gold top and bottom borders, then the side borders. Press seams toward borders.

8. Layer your quilt top with the batting and backing. Pin or thread-baste the layers together.

9. Stitch in-the-ditch around the major shapes. Use straight stitching about ½" apart to echo quilt around the horses. Internal quilted lines, spaced about ½" apart, were also added between the satin stitched lines on the horses. Bind or finish as desired.

HEART
FILLED
WITH
LOVE

LIVE
FROM
THE
WISE
VOICE
IN
YOUR
HEART,
AND
EACH
DAY
WILL
BLOSSOM
@

Laurel

Who wouldn't love to receive this as a true gift from the heart? You can experiment with painting and stamping techniques while creating a wonderful assortment of Laurel's kindred creatures.

HEART FILLED WITH LOVE

Finished Framed Size: 36" x 30"
Machine appliquéd and quilted by Lynn Koolish, Berkeley, California, 2001.
Fabric generously donated by Robert Kaufman Co., Inc.

MATERIALS

♥ Light yellow: 1 yard for the background (or 1½ yards if quilt will have binding rather than a frame)

♥ Scraps of the following: assorted greens, blues, pinks, yellows, oranges, purples, black

♥ Backing: 1 yard light-colored fabric

♥ Batting: 40" x 34"

♥ Fusible web: 2 yards

♥ Tear-away stabilizer: 2 yards

♥ Threads for decorative stitching: metalic gold, black, turquoise

♥ Fabric paint: assorted colors including black and white

♥ Assorted beads and buttons

TIPS FOR MAKING HEART FILLED WITH LOVE

1. Have the pattern enlarged 260% before you begin, overlapping the two sections. See instructions for machine appliqué using fusible web on page 87.

2. Cover your workspace to protect it before you begin to paint. Do all of your painting before you fuse pieces to the background. If you make any painting mistakes, you can just re-paint a piece. Lightly draw in all of the details, such as the scallop design on the bird's wing. Several techniques were used to paint the pieces including sponging, stamping, and brushing. For more tips see page 88.

In this project, all of the pieces were fused to the background prior to doing any stitching.

3. Pin or baste a large piece of the tear-away stabilizer behind the quilt top. Start sewing the decorative stitching on the shapes that fall under another layer, such as the leaves under the cat's body.

Note that some shapes are outlined with two colors, usually along the outer edge. Satin stitching was used for outlining; straight stitching was used for details like whiskers, antennae, and outlines of feathers. Tapering the satin stitching at the points of leaves, bird beak, and other pointed shapes will lend a refined quality to the quilt.

4. Layer your quilt top with the batting and backing. Pin or thread baste the layers together.

5. Quilt around the animals with clear monofilament thread. Embellish with beads and buttons.

6. This project was finished with a mat board and frame. If you prefer, you can cut the quilt into a heart shape and bind with bias binding that matches the background fabric.

A straight stitch was used to outline the feathers.

Beads add a great decorative detail.

heart filled with love pattern

RAINBOW FRIENDS

I want to
capture the
brilliant
rainbow
Colors
of the world
and its creatures...
painting images
that express
the magic of
special
friendships,
and
Celebrate Life!
...images that
remind us of
our connectedness
to the sacred
places within
ourselves and
each other...

Laurel

Laurel Burch

RAINBOW FRIENDS

Finished Quilt Size: 25" x 32"
Machine appliquéd and quilted by Michele Crawford,
Spokane, Washington, 2001.
Fabric generously donated by the Robert Kaufman Company.

MATERIALS

- ♥ Yellow: 1½ yards for borders, horse's head and body, and backing
- ♥ Fuchsia: ¼ yard for border, horse's face/mane, part of the bird's body, and part of dog's face
- ♥ Dark blue-purple: ⅜ yard for borders, dog's ears/nose unit, stripes on dog's body, and cat eyebrows
- ♥ Turquoise: ⅜ yard for cat's body, triangles on border, part of bird, horse's mane
- ♥ Red-purple: ⅜ yard for dog's body and binding
- ♥ Orange-yellow: ¾ yard for background, border, bird's beak, part of horse's mane, and circles on top and bottom borders
- ♥ Scraps of the following: Light blue-violet for cat's cheeks, rusty red for horse's ears and the bird, lime green for bird's head, light blue for bird's head, coral for cat's eyes, white for eyes
- ♥ Batting: 29" x 36"
- ♥ Fusible web: 2 yards
- ♥ Tear-away stabilizer: 1 yard
- ♥ Thread for decorative stitching: black, turquoise, yellow
- ♥ Fabric paint: black and gold "puff" paint for dots in borders, and for outlining triangles and circles in borders
- ♥ Gold cording: 3½ yards (for either side of yellow borders)
- ♥ Small black beads for eyes

CUTTING

Yellow:
Inner border: Cut two strips 1"-wide x 29½".
Backing: Cut one 29" x 36" rectangle.

Orange-yellow:
Left side border: Cut one strip 2¼"-wide x 29½".
Background: Cut one 15" x 32" rectangle.

Fuchsia:
Right side border: Cut one strip 5¾"-wide x 29½".

Dark blue-purple:
Outer side borders: Cut two strips 2½"-wide x 32".
Top border: Cut one strip 1½"-wide x 21".
Bottom border: Cut one strip 2"-wide x 21".

Red-purple:
Binding: Cut three strips 2¼"-wide x width of fabric.

TIPS FOR MAKING RAINBOW FRIENDS

1. Have the pattern enlarged 350% before you begin. See instructions for machine appliqué using fusible web on page 87. Assemble the center with all of the "friends" first.

2. Cover your workspace to protect it before you begin to paint any of the internal details, such as the eyes. Paint before you start fusing appliqué shapes to the background. Let paint dry completely. Do not use puff paint for these internal details. Please note that the painted outlines around the triangles and circles in the borders and the dots on the yellow and orange-yellow borders are added as a last step after the quilt has been quilted and bound.

3. Cut all shapes and fuse in place. Note that a large rectangle was used for the background. The ears, facial details, and left side of the horse's head were fused onto the yellow horse's body.

The stripes on the dog's body were fused onto the red-purple body.

4. Lightly draw in the details that will be stitched, such as the whiskers. Pin or baste the tear-away stabilizer to the back of the panel. Satin stitch around all of the raw edges.

5. Trim the center to 13" × 29½" after the appliqué is complete.

6. Sew the left side yellow inner border strip to the orange-yellow border strip with the gold cording sandwiched in between. Add to the left side of the background with another strip of gold cording sandwiched in between. Press seams toward the borders.

7. Sew the yellow right side inner border strip to the fuchsia border strip with gold cording sandwiched between borders. Add to the right side of the background with gold cording sandwiched in between. Press seams toward the borders.

8. Fuse the turquoise triangles to the dark blue-purple outer side borders. (Paint is added after the entire quilt has been sewn together and pressed.) For the bottom dark blue-purple border circles, fuse the fuchsia inner circles to the orange-yellow outer circles, then fuse to the bottom border. Fuse the orange-yellow circles to the top border. Add the borders to the quilt top and bottom first, then outer sides. Press seams toward the borders.

9. Layer your quilt top with the batting and backing. Pin or thread baste the layers together.

10. Stitch in-the-ditch around all of the major shapes and between borders. The fuchsia border is a great place to add other quilted "creatures" found throughout the book. Bind or finish as desired.

11. Add the painted details last. These include gold dots under the horse's eyes and on the cat's body, tiny black dots in the orange and yellow borders, and gold around the circles and triangles in the borders. Black beads were sewn on for most of the eyes; a gold bead was used for the bird's eye.

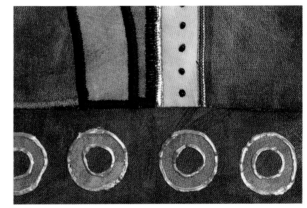

Border details

magic is captured
in the eyes of these

dream Believers.

they've come
     to sweep you away
        to a mythical place
              where
(IF YOU Believe...!)
     all things are possible
     when you follow
       your own special
          passions and dreams.

                    laurel

This twin-bed sized quilt would add a fanciful burst of color to any bedroom; it could also be used as a wonderful wallhanging on a larger wall. If you can't find printed fabrics similar to the prints used in this quilt, consider doing some fabric stamping on solid fabrics to create your own printed fabric.

Center of quilt

DREAM BELIEVERS

Finished Quilt Size: 67½" x 93½"
Machine appliquéd, pieced, and quilted by Barbara Baker and Jeri Boe, Bend, Oregon, 2000.
Fabric generously donated by Marcus Brothers.

MATERIALS

♥ Turquoise: 3 yards for horse's body, fish, borders

♥ Yellow: 1⅝ yards for background, bird, fish, borders

♥ Yellow print: ⅓ yard for borders

♥ Large black print: 1½ yards for cat's body, borders

♥ Small black print: 1 yard for borders

♥ Blue print: ⅝ yard for mouse's body and borders

♥ Red with yellow stars: ⅜ yard for cat's body

♥ Orange/yellow print: ½ yard for borders

♥ Orange print: ⅜ yard for cat's face, fish, and borders

♥ Fuchsia: ½ yard for borders

♥ Green print: ½ yard for fish and borders

♥ Purple: ½ yard for mouse's face and borders

♥ Black: ¾ yard for binding, cat's ears and nose

♥ Red: ½ yard for cat's ears, nose, and borders

♥ Scraps of various prints for birds and fish

♥ Backing: 5½ yards

♥ Batting: 71" x 97"

♥ Fusible web: 3 yards

♥ Tear-away stabilizer: 3 yards

♥ Thread for decorative stitching: black and yellow

♥ Fabric paint: white, black, and bright blue

CUTTING

See the dimensions in the cutting and assembly diagram on page 52; these are the sizes to cut and include the seam allowances. We recommend you cut the background for the center panel slightly larger than the size given, then trim to the size shown after the appliqué is complete.

Binding: Cut nine strips 2¼"-wide.

Embellishing details

TIPS FOR MAKING DREAM BELIEVERS

1. Have the pattern on page 52 enlarged 550% before you begin. See instructions for machine appliqué using fusible web on page 87. Assemble the center panel first.

2. Cover your workspace to protect it. Add the painted and stitched details before fusing. The eyes on all of the creatures, the teeth on the horse, and the dots were painted. Let paint dry completely before you begin fusing.

3. Cut all shapes for the center panel and fuse them in place.

4. Thread or pin-baste tear-away stabilizer onto the individual pieces, such as the different fish, and add satin stitching. Trim the center panel to 39" x 43½".

5. Add the borders used to frame the center panel according to the cutting and assembly diagram on page 53.

6. Add the top and bottom units to the center panel, then the side units.

7. Layer your quilt top with the batting and backing. Pin or thread baste the layers together.

8. Stitch in-the-ditch around all of the creatures, between borders, etc. Outline quilt ¼" away from border seams. Use a large meandering stitch to quilt the borders and around the creatures. Bind or finish as desired.

Dream Believers Cutting and Assembly Diagram

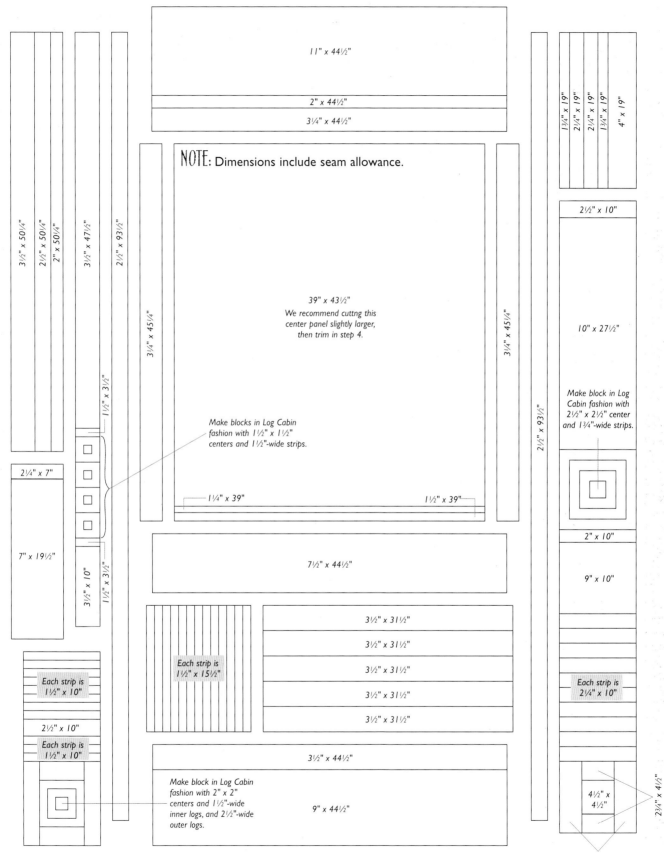

11" x 44½"

2" x 44½"

3¼" x 44½"

1¾" x 19"
2¼" x 19"
2¼" x 19"
1¾" x 19"
4" x 19"

3½" x 50¼"
2½" x 50¼"
2" x 50¼"

3½" x 47½"

2¼" x 93½"

2½" x 10"

NOTE: Dimensions include seam allowance.

3¼" x 45¼"

3¼" x 45¼"

10" x 27½"

39" x 43½"
We recommend cuttng this
center panel slightly larger,
then trim in step 4.

Make block in Log
Cabin fashion with
2½" x 2½" center
and 1¾"-wide strips.

1½" x 3½"

Make blocks in Log Cabin
fashion with 1½" x 1½"
centers and 1½"-wide strips.

2½" x 93½"

1¼" x 39"

1½" x 39"

2¼" x 7"

7" x 19½"

3½" x 10"

1½" x 3½"

7½" x 44½"

2" x 10"

9" x 10"

3½" x 31½"

3½" x 31½"

3½" x 31½"

3½" x 31½"

3½" x 31½"

Each strip is
1½" x 15½"

Each strip is
2¼" x 10"

Each strip is
1½" x 10"

2½" x 10"

Each strip is
1½" x 10"

3½" x 44½"

Make block in Log Cabin
fashion with 2" x 2"
centers and 1½"-wide
inner logs, and 2½"-wide
outer logs.

9" x 44½"

4½" x
4½"

2¾" x 4½"

3¼" x 9"

53

MYTHICAL
DOGS

MYTHICAL DOGS

Finished Quilt Size: 42½" x 50¾"
Machine appliquéd, pieced, and quilted by Cyndy Lyle Rymer, Danville, California, 2001.
Fabric generously donated by Hoffman California Fabrics.

MATERIALS

▼ A variety of fat quarters (to total 2½ yards) can be used for this project. Choose from green, fuchsia, turquoise, orange, gold, blue, and purple.

▼ Background: six different fat quarters, or 1½ yards of a single fabric if you want to use just one fabric for all of the blocks

▼ Borders: ¼ yard each of two different fabrics

▼ Backing: 2 yards

▼ Batting: 46" x 55"

▼ Binding: ½ yard

▼ Fusible web: 3 yards

▼ Tear-away stabilizer: 3 yards

▼ Threads for decorative stitching: black, metallic gold

▼ Fabric paint: turquoise, gold, white, black, fuchsia

CUTTING

See the dimensions in the cutting and assembly diagram on page 58; these are the sizes to cut and include the seam allowances. We recommend you cut the block backgrounds larger than the sizes given, then trim to the size shown after the appliqué is complete.

For the 8 half-square triangles in the quilt body: Cut eight 2⅞" squares, then cut in half diagonally.

For the 18 half-square triangles in the borders: Cut eighteen 4⅞" squares, then cut in half diagonally.

Binding: Cut five strips 2¼"-wide x width of the fabric .

TIPS FOR MAKING MYTHICAL DOGS

1. Have the dog patterns you plan to use enlarged 250% before you begin. See instructions for machine appliqué using fusible web on page 87.

2. The method of putting the quilt top together is your choice. You can work on each dog block individually and then stitch them all together, or you can sew all of the background together and then add the dogs.

Please note: Just like dogs who won't stay in their own yards, parts of some of these dogs, such as heads and tails, stray outside their background blocks onto other blocks, or sashing and border strips. See step 5 below for fusing techniques.

3. Cover your workspace to protect it before you begin to paint or stamp. See page 89 for painting tips. Stamp the various shapes on the background rectangles, but you don't need to stamp in the centers because they will be covered by the dog's bodies.

Stamp shapes as desired on the dog bodies. Additional color can be added by sponging on fabric paint. Let paint dry completely before you fuse any shapes onto the backgrounds.

Detail of stamping and stitching

4. Cut out all shapes, and lightly draw in details such as the internal curve of a dog's leg, or the nose lines.

5. As mentioned above, most of the dogs' bodies overlap adjoining parts of the quilt top. Fuse only part of the body to its background block. Leave the paper backing on the fusible web on the part(s) of the body that will be fused after all the pieces are joined together. Remember to fold and pin the unattached part of the body away from the seam allowance before joining rows.

6. Thread or pin-baste tear-away stabilizer onto the individual blocks (or quilt top, depending on your method of assembly) and satin stitch around all the raw edges. Use a narrower satin stitch for outlining the internal body parts.

In spots where body parts overlap another background block, you will have to wait to complete not only the fusing, but the outline stitching as well, until the dog is completely fused to the sewn rows.

7. Make eight 2⅞" half-square triangle units shown in the quilt diagram. Follow the cutting and assembly diagram for placement.

Make eighteen 4⅞" half-square triangle units for the top and bottom borders. Sew together two borders of nine half-square triangle blocks each.

Piece the remaining units before putting together the quilt top following the cutting and assembly diagram.

8. Layer your quilt top with the batting and backing. Pin or thread baste the layers together.

9. Stitch in-the-ditch around all of the dogs and in between all of the stripped units and half-square triangles. You can also echo quilt around all of the dogs. Bind or finish as desired.

Mythical Dogs Cutting and Assembly Diagram

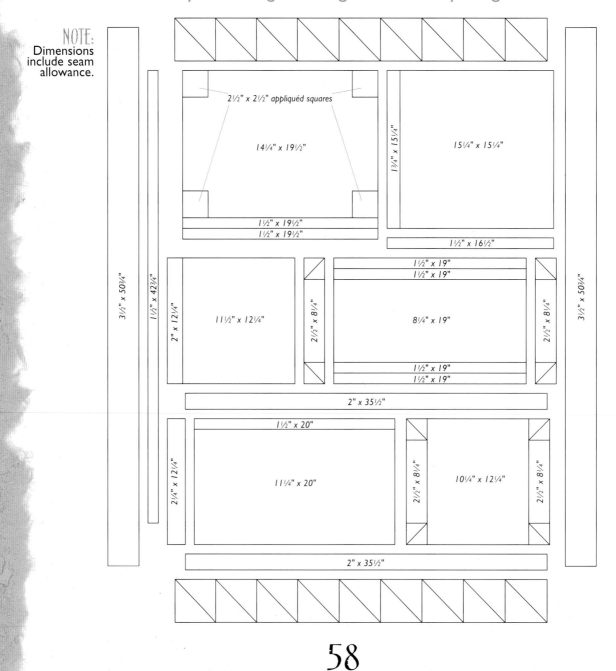

NOTE:
Dimensions include seam allowance.

2½" x 2½" appliquéd squares

14¼" x 19½"

1¾" x 15¼"

15¼" x 15¼"

1½" x 19½"
1½" x 19½"

1½" x 16½"

3½" x 50¾"

1½" x 42¼"

2" x 12¼"

11½" x 12¼"

2½" x 8¼"

1½" x 19"
1½" x 19"

8¼" x 19"

2½" x 8¼"

3½" x 50¾"

1½" x 19"
1½" x 19"

2" x 35½"

1½" x 20"

2¼" x 12¼"

11¼" x 20"

2½" x 8¼"

10¼" x 12¼"

2½" x 8¼"

2" x 35½"

basso and corazón patterns

FELINE FAIRIES

Laurel Burch

close your eyes
and dream a dream...
    and seek the courage
 to make it real.

reflect on the past.
  envision the future,
 embrace today with passion

laurel

FELINE FAIRIES

Finished Quilt Size: 36¼" x 48"
Machine appliquéd, pieced, and quilted by
Nancy Odom, Westfield, Indiana, 2000.
Fabric generously donated by Hoffman California Fabrics.

MATERIALS

♥ Black: 3¼ yards for background, backing, and binding
♥ Scraps or a variety of fat quarters to total 3 yards can be used for this project. Choose dark green, navy, light turquoise, orange, gold, magenta, light violet, and purple.
♥ Border: ¼ yard each of two different fabrics
♥ Batting: 40" x 52"
♥ Fusible web: 2½ yards
♥ Tear-away stabilizer: 2½ yards
♥ Threads for decorative stitching: black, turquoise, metallic gold, white, black, fuchsia, yellow, violet, green
♥ Fabric paint: black, turquoise, gold metallic, white, yellow, red
♥ Fabric pen: gold

CUTTING

See the dimensions in the cutting and assembly diagram on page 68; these are the sizes to cut and include the seam allowances. We recommend you cut the block backgrounds larger than the sizes given, then trim to the size shown after the appliqué is complete.

For the lower side border: cut ten 1¾" squares.

For the upper side border: cut seven triangles 2" high with a base of 1⅜".

For the larger half-square triangles in the top and bottom borders: Cut twenty-two 3⅝" squares of various colors, then cut in half diagonally.

For the smaller half-square triangles in the quilt body: Cut four 3⅜" squares of various colors, then cut in half diagonally.

Binding: Cut five strips 2¼"-wide x width of the fabric.

TIPS FOR MAKING FELINE FAIRIES

1. You will need to enlarge the pattern for each Feline Fairy you plan to use. See pages 69-74 for enlargement instructions. See instructions for machine appliqué using fusible web on page 87.

The method of putting the quilt top together is your choice. You can work on each cat block individually and then stitch them all together, or you can sew the entire background together and then add the cats.

2. Cut out all shapes, and lightly draw in details. Cover your workspace to protect it before you begin to stamp or paint. See page 89 for painting tips. Paint each cat layer individually, and let dry completely. Fuse all parts together.

Paint or stamp hearts on the four squares in the upper left block and outline with gold fabric pen. These squares are appliquéd onto the quilt top.

Paint the black background with spirals, stars, and layers of circles and dots.

3. Most of the cats' bodies overlap adjoining parts of the quilt top. Fuse only part of the body to its background block. Leave the paper backing on the fusible web on the part(s) of the body that will be fused after all the pieces are joined together. Remember to fold and pin the unattached part of the body away from the seam allowance before joining rows.

4. Thread or pin-baste tear-away stabilizer onto the individual blocks (or quilt top, depending on your method of assembly) and satin stitch around all the raw edges.

5. Make 22 half-square triangle units for the top and bottom borders. Sew twelve half-square triangle units together for the top border. Sew eight units together to use in the bottom border. Follow the cutting and assembly diagram for the rest of the bottom border.

66

Piece the remaining units before putting together the quilt top following the cutting and assembly diagram.

6. Use the smaller half-square triangles to make four units. Trim two units to 2½" square—these are appliquéd onto the top of the bottom left rectangle.

7. Note that the smaller squares within the lower side border squares were painted on, then outlined with a black or metallic gold fabric pen. As a final touch small white painted dots were added. Let all paint dry completely before appliquéing the squares onto the left border.

8. Piece the remaining units before putting together the quilt top following the cutting and assembly diagram.

9. If you used the blanket stitch on the raw edges, outline each cat with gold metallic fabric pen. Add whiskers and other details with black or gold metallic fabric pen.

10. Layer your quilt top with the batting and backing. Pin or thread baste the layers together.

11. Stitch in-the-ditch around all of the cats, the hearts, and in between all of the stripped units and half-square triangles. Bind or finish as desired.

67

Feline Fairies Cutting and Assembly Diagram

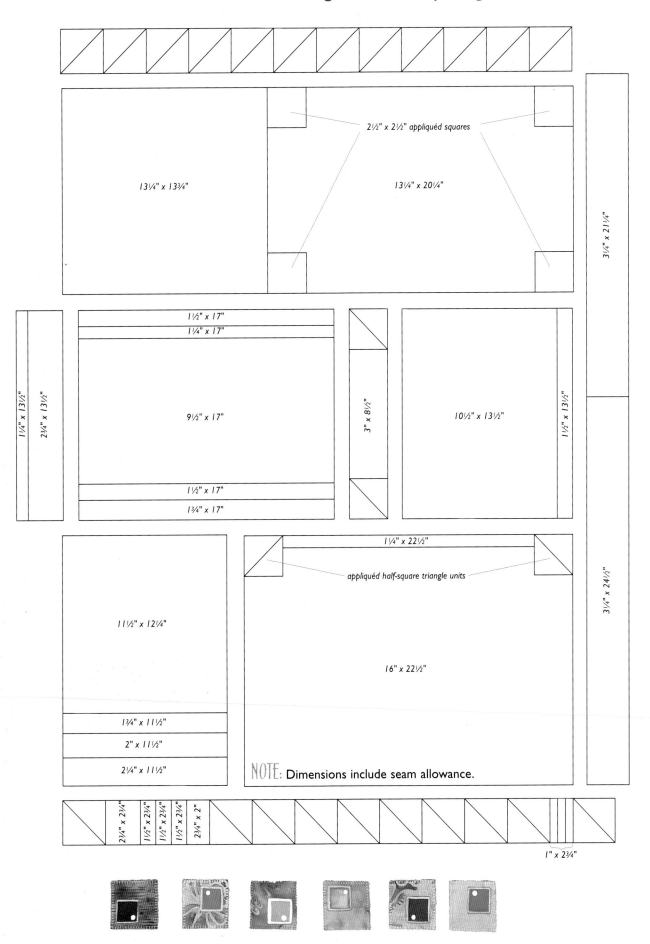

13¼" x 13¾"

2½" x 2½" appliquéd squares

13¼" x 20¼"

3¼" x 21¼"

1½" x 17"
1¼" x 17"

1¼" x 13½"
2¾" x 13½"

9½" x 17"

3" x 8½"

10½" x 13½"

1½" x 13½"

1½" x 17"
1¾" x 17"

1¼" x 22½"

appliquéd half-square triangle units

11½" x 12¼"

16" x 22½"

3¼" x 24½"

1¾" x 11½"

2" x 11½"

2¼" x 11½"

NOTE: Dimensions include seam allowance.

2¾" x 2¾"
1½" x 2¾"
1½" x 2¾"
1½" x 2¾"
2¾" x 2"

1" x 2¾"

angelica's pattern

Enlarge pattern 175%

69

Enlarge pattern 150%

Enlarge pattern 200%

kit's pattern

Enlarge pattern 150%

Enlarge pattern 240%

angelino's pattern

Enlarge pattern 185%

KINDRED CREATURES

Laurel Burch

A multitude of kindred spirits come together to grace this quilt. This project would make an incredibly special gift for the person or people who are closest to your heart. As Laurel says, "Each piece of art fulfills its greatest purpose when it enhances a person's life or finds its home in someone's heart. The magic continues when this feeling is shared with a loved one or friend."

KINDRED CREATURES

Finished Quilt Size: 30½" square
Machine appliquéd and quilted by Nancy Odom, Westfield, Indiana, 2000.
Fabrics generously donated by Timeless Treasures Fabrics, Inc. from the Patrick Lose collection.

MATERIALS

- ♥ Black: 2 yards for background, backing, and facings
- ♥ Light purple: ¼ yard for horse and border
- ♥ Red: ¼ yard for borders and flowers
- ♥ Turquoise: ⅜ yard for wild dog
- ♥ Orange: ½ yard for jackal (on right) and border
- ♥ Fuchsia: ½ yard for cat and border
- ♥ Fat quarters of violet, yellow, and two to three different greens
- ♥ Scraps of dark blue-purple
- ♥ Batting: 34" × 34"
- ♥ Fusible web: 3 yards
- ♥ Tear-away stabilizer: 2½ yards
- ♥ Threads for decorative stitching: gold metallic, black, turquoise, greens, pink, yellow, orange
- ♥ Small purple buttons for large red flower
- ♥ Black and gold beads

CUTTING

See the dimensions in the cutting and assembly diagram on page 79; these are the sizes to cut and include the seam allowances.

Black:

Background: Cut one 25" × 23" rectangle (will be trimmed after appliqué is complete).
Facings: Cut two 1¾" × 30½" strips for side facings.
Cut two 1¾" × 31½" strips for top and bottom facings.

TIPS FOR MAKING KINDRED CREATURES

1. Trace all pattern pieces onto the fusible web following the instructions on page 87. (A full-size pattern pullout can be found in the back of the book.)

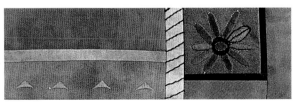

Embroidery details

2. All of the details in this quilt were machine embroidered onto the individual parts before being fused to the background, including the details on the flower petals, dots on the borders, the flowers in the corners of the borders, and the black stripes in the yellow borders. You can choose to paint or appliqué rather than embroider the details.

3. Pin or thread-baste the tear-away stabilizer to the back of any piece before you begin stitching.

4. One suggestion is to put larger pieces, such as the cat, in an embroidery hoop, stitch the interior details, and then cut out appliqué shapes afterwards. Once these are cut out, place the shapes on the background for fusing.

5. Leave the paper backing of the fusible web on the appliqué pieces that overlap the borders—the fuchsia cat and the jackal's tail—until the borders have been attached. Pin these parts of the quilt away from the seam allowance. Carefully fuse the creatures to the background. Trim the center panel to 23½" wide × 21½" high.

6. Piece the border strips together according to the cutting and assembly diagram.

A note about the flower units in the corners: If you can't find gold metallic fabric, you can paint a different color fabric with metallic gold paint. Heat set it before doing any embroidery.

7. Fuse the remaining part of the fuchsia cat and the jackal's tail to the quilt top.

8. Pin or thread baste the tear-away stabilizer to the quilt top, and satin stitch around all of the raw edges.

9. Layer your quilt top with the batting and backing. Pin or thread baste the layers together.

10. Stitch in-the-ditch around all of the animals, the flowers, parts of the leaves, and in between all of the borders.

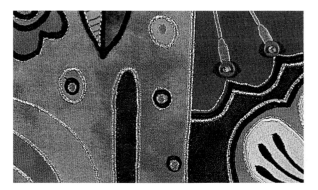
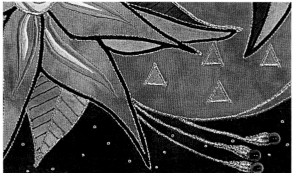

11. This is another great opportunity for beading: gold seed beads were added to the background, black seed beads were used under the cat's and jackal's eyes, and in the middles of the flowers. You can use beads as the dots on the birds. Small purple buttons and yellow beads were used in the large red flower to the right of the fuchsia cat.

12. Note that this project was finished with facings to provide a clean finish. However, you can bind or finish as desired.

Kindred Creatures Cutting and Assembly Diagram

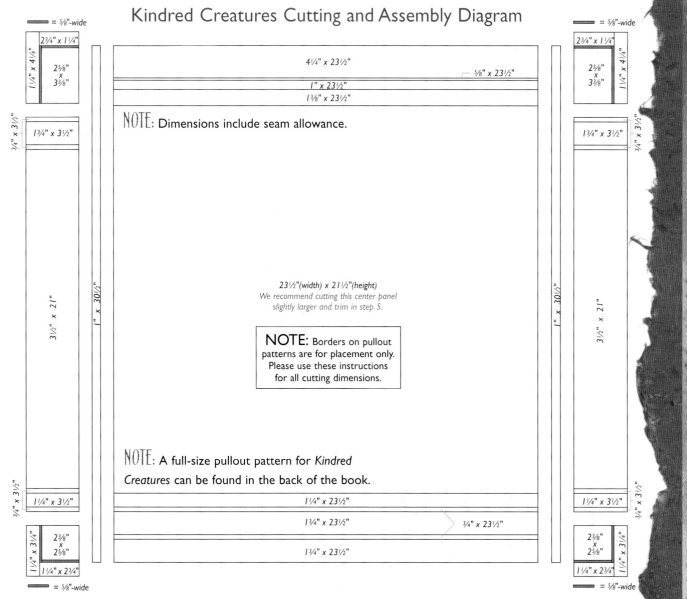

= ⅝"-wide

2¾" x 1¼"

1¼" x 4¼"

2⅝" x 3⅜"

¾" x 3½"

1¾" x 3½"

3½" x 21"

1" x 30½"

¾" x 3½"

1¼" x 3½"

1¼" x 3¼"

2⅜" x 2⅝"

1¼" x 2¾"

= ⅝"-wide

4¼" x 23½"

⅝" x 23½"

1" x 23½"

1⅜" x 23½"

NOTE: Dimensions include seam allowance.

23½"(width) x 21½"(height)
We recommend cutting this center panel
slightly larger and trim in step 5.

NOTE: Borders on pullout
patterns are for placement only.
Please use these instructions
for all cutting dimensions.

NOTE: A full-size pullout pattern for Kindred
Creatures can be found in the back of the book.

1¼" x 23½"

1¾" x 23½"

¾" x 23½"

1¾" x 23½"

= ⅝"-wide

2¾" x 1¼"

1¼" x 4¼"

2⅝" x 3⅜"

1¾" x 3½"

1" x 30½"

3½" x 21"

1¼" x 3½"

2⅜" x 2⅝"

1¼" x 2¾"

= ⅝"-wide

CARLOTTA
IN THE
SECRET
GARDEN

As a child
i was sure
i was a "Secret Garden
Fairy" that no one but
garden creatures and
flowers could see.

i made little flower bud
wreathes for my hair
and sat on the rocks
among my gramma Lillian's
Gigantic flowers ...
catching baby frogs
and iridescent dragonflies
to talk to.

The magic of those summer
days stays with me always,
and comes alive here in this painting
as a way of sharing these
memories with you ♥

laurel

CARLOTTA IN THE SECRET GARDEN

Finished Quilt Size: 40¾" x 29½"
Machine appliquéd and quilted by Barbara Baker and Jeri Boe, Bend, Oregon, 2000.
Fabrics generously donated by Hoffman California Fabrics.

MATERIALS

♥ Beige: 1 yard for background
♥ Checked fabrics: ⅛ yard each small and large checked fabrics for borders
♥ Scraps or a variety of fat quarters—approximately 22 different fabrics—can be used for this project. Suggested fabrics include batiks and hand-dyed fabrics.
♥ Choose from the following color families:
Black for Carlotta's body and the lower half of her face, dark gray for the top half of Carlotta's face. For the flowers and leaves choose a variety of colors: yellow, magenta, gold, four to five different greens, fuchsia, orange, blue, teal, purple, red
♥ Backing: 1¼ yards
♥ Batting: 43" x 33"
♥ Binding: ⅜ yard
♥ Fusible web: 3 yards
♥ Tear-away stabilizer: 3 yards
♥ Threads for decorative stitching: metallic gold, black, fuchsia, tan, orange, red, royal blue, yellow
♥ Fabric paints: gold metallic, lilac, white, blue, and black
♥ Iron-on crayons (optional)
♥ Assorted beads (purples, reds, blues, etc.)

CUTTING

Beige:

Background: Cut one 36" x 27" rectangle (will be trimmed after appliqué is complete).

BORDERS

Top inner border

Teal blue: Cut one strip 1¼"-wide x 1½".
Small gold check: Cut one strip 1¼"-wide x 23".
Yellow: Cut one strip 1¼"-wide x 11".

> **NOTE:** Borders on pullout patterns are for placement only. Please use these instructions for all cutting dimensions.

Right side inner border

Yellow: Cut one strip 1¼"-wide x 6½".
Gold check: Cut one strip 1¼"-wide x 20½".

Bottom inner border

Larger gold check: Cut one strip 1"-wide x 34½".

Left side inner border

Larger gold check: Cut one strip 1½"-wide x 22¼".
Teal blue: Cut one strip 1½"-wide x 4¾".

Top outer border

Fuchsia print: Cut one strip 2"-wide x 23½".
Orange: Cut one strip 2"-wide x 13¼".
Lighter orange: Cut one strip 2"-wide x 5".

Right outer border

Gold: Cut one strip 2¾"-wide x 20½".
Yellow: Cut one strip 2¾"-wide x 8".

Bottom outer border

Yellow: Cut one strip 2"-wide x 3½".
Teal blue: Cut one strip 2"-wide x 23¼".
Purple: Cut one strip 2"-wide x 10½".

Left outer border

Purple: Cut one strip 2¾"-wide x 28".
Binding: Cut four strips 2¼"-wide x width of the fabric.

Embellishing details

84

TIPS FOR MAKING
CARLOTTA IN THE SECRET GARDEN

1. Trace all pattern pieces onto the fusible web following the instructions on page 87. (A full-size pattern can be found in the back of the book.)

2. Cover your workspace to protect it before you begin to paint, stencil, or stamp any details. Let dry completely.

The checked borders shown were made using a black and white print with iron-on crayons. See page 89 for hints on using fabric crayons.

3. Layer the individual flowers and Carlotta's face. Place all shapes on the background, and check to make sure there are no gaps or open spaces. If so, you can cover them with a small piece of fabric. Fuse everything in place.

4. Back the quilt top with tear-away stabilizer. Start in the center for the satin stitching and work out toward the borders. This is a great opportunity to listen to a book on tape while you work, because the satin stitching does take some time.

Details of stitching and painting

5. Once the center panel is complete, trim it to 34½" × 25¼", keeping the design centered.

Piece the border strips together in the order shown on the pattern, checking against the photo of the quilt as you go. Add the top and bottom inner borders first, then the side inner borders. Press seams toward the borders. Next add the bottom outer border, then the side borders, and finally the top border. Press seams toward the borders.

6. Layer your quilt top with the batting and backing. Pin or thread baste the layers together.

7. Stitch in-the-ditch around Carlotta's body and facial features and around all of the flowers and leaves. Use a meandering quilting stitch in the borders.

8. If you enjoy beading, the flowers in this quilt are wonderful areas for showcasing your talents. Bind or finish as desired.

Details of beading

NOTE: A full-size pullout pattern for *Carlotta in the Secret Garden* can be found in the back of the book.

TIPS & TECHNIQUES

SUGGESTED FABRICS

All of the projects in this book were made with 100% cotton fabrics. Most people will find these the easiest to work with and they are widely available.

RECOMMENDED
TYPES OF COTTON ARE:

Batiks

Marbled

Hand-dyed

Small abstract prints

Geometric prints

Solids

Please note that while we give you the enlargement percentage we used to create the projects you can make your project larger or smaller simply by adjusting the enlargement percentage.

Laurel's quilts provide a great opportunity to use your favorite fabrics.

PREPARING TO APPLIQUÉ

HAND APPLIQUÉ

Traditional needle-turn appliqué techniques can be used for most projects in this book. In the *Summer Flutter-bye* even the small metallic dots were hand appliquéd on as small circles. If you would like to create any of the projects using traditional appliqué methods, you only need to remember to add ⅛" to ¼" seam allowances around all pattern pieces. Remember that you can still experiment with painting, stamping, and decorative stitching. The amount of embellishment you choose to add to each project is a personal decision.

MACHINE APPLIQUÉ

Most of the projects in this book were made using machine appliqué techniques. Read through all the project instructions carefully before you begin a project. Most of the patterns need to be enlarged before you start to work. The pullouts at the back of the book for *Carlotta in the Secret Garden* and *Kindred Creatures* are full-size patterns that can be used as is. Take the other patterns you want to work with to a photocopy center and ask that they enlarge them to the percentage suggested for each project. In some cases, the patterns will have to be enlarged in a two-step process, and therefore may cost a little more.

General Appliqué Procedures

To help place the pieces on your background fabric, trace the key lines (the black lines on the patterns) onto the background fabric using a pencil or thin permanent pen. If you have a light box or a bright window, you can use it to trace the outlines onto the fabric. Another method is to periodically place the background fabric directly over the drawing and position the fabric pieces as you work. If you are working with a light background fabric, you should be able to see the major outlines without a lightbox. If you are using dark fabric for your background, you can transfer the key lines with sewing tracing paper and a tracing wheel.

Fabric key for Mariah Moonbeam and Friend

Study the pattern and plan how you are going to layer the pieces. Working from the bottom layer to the top layer, think about which pieces will go under other pieces. A suggestion: Make a photocopy of the pattern and jot down notes to yourself about the layering order. Make sure that you overlap dark colored pieces over lighter pieces—if you overlap a light color over a dark color, you will see a "shadow" from the dark piece underneath. As you cut out your fabric pieces, it will be helpful to mark the points where they overlap.

You may also want to create a "fabric key" to help you remember where you are planning to use your different fabrics.

Trace the pattern pieces to the wrong/rough side (not the paper side) of a lightweight paper-backed fusible web using a permanent pen. (If you prefer drawing on the paper side of the fusible web, you will need to reverse the drawing that you are tracing. You can have this done at a photocopy center.) Add at least a ¼" seam allowance for pieces that are going to be tucked under another piece. For larger pieces, to avoid bulk you may want to cut away the inside of the fusible web, leaving a ½" outline. (Use the cut-away interfacing for smaller shapes.)

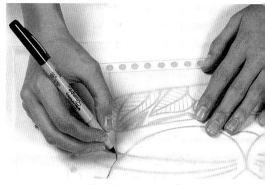

Transferring the design

Fuse the web to the wrong side of the selected fabric. Mark the edges that will be tucked under. Be sure to follow the manufacturer's instructions when fusing. You can either fuse all the pieces at once, filling in any gaps as needed, or you can fuse and stitch as you go. Note that in some places where shapes extend into borders or neighboring blocks, you will need to keep the paper backing on, pin that part away from the rest of it, and finish fusing after the entire quilt top has been sewn together.

After stitching pieces that will be layered, cut away the underneath layer of fabric to prevent fabric build up. Try not to have more than two layers of fabric on top of each other.

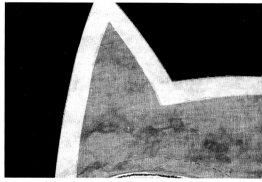

Cut away the inside of large pieces of fusible web to reduce bulk and stiffness.

PRESSING TIP Use a non-stick pressing cloth to keep your iron and ironing board clean. If you do get some of the fusible adhesive on your iron, clean it off with iron cleaner before you continue working, or you will get the adhesive on your work.

Use the pattern to check placement
of shapes to be appliquéd.

Dots were made with the eraser end of a fat pencil.

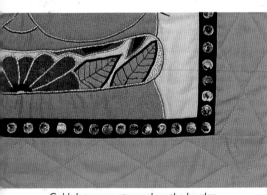

Gold dots were stamped on the border
before it was sewn to the center panel.

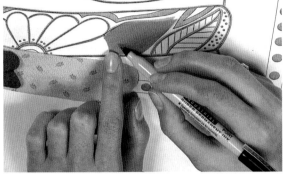

To make it easier to stitch
or paint, mark details such
as whiskers, flutter-bye
antennae, leaf veins, leaf
petals, and so on with pencil
or thin permanent pen.

Using a lightbox for tracing helps. As an alternative, for tracing small areas, you can make your own "lightbox" with a piece of glass or plastic and a light bulb underneath or you can use a plexiglass quilting extension if you have one. Taping the original pattern on a large window, then taping the base layer on top, also works.

PAINTING AND DRAWING

STAMPING

Stamps can be purchased (see Resources) or you can make them yourself from sheets of art foam or erasers. A pencil eraser is great for dots; a fatter pencil can be used for the larger dots such as the purple dots on the Flutter-bye wings.

Susan Hagen, a fabric stamping teacher from Walnut Creek, California, offers the following tips for fabric stamping:

1. "Rough up" a new fabric stamp (not stamps made for paper) with fine sandpaper before you use it.

2. Shake the jar of paint before using it, then dab the tip of your foam paintbrush into the cap. This eliminates the need for a paint palette and prevents the brush from becoming overly saturated.

3. Put a thin coat of paint onto the stamp, using a foam paint brush.

4. Pad your workspace with a piece of cardboard or a few layers of fabric to get a good stamped image.

5. Stamp the image firmly onto the fabric and rock the stamp slightly for a clear image.

6. If you get excess paint on the stamp use a cotton swab to wipe it off. Clean out small details with a toothpick.

7. Heat set the paint following the manufacturer's instructions.

8. To clean your stamps, use a nail brush or old toothbrush under running water.

There are several types of stamps you can try: sponge stamps, foam stamps, and harder rubber stamps. They will all give you different results, so experiment with each to see which type you want to use.

Different types of stamps give different results.

BRUSHING

Fine point brushes are great for creating lines, spirals, small dots, and other decorative shapes. Use a plate or other flat surface for a palette. Practice on a scrap of fabric first.

SPONGING

There may be areas where you want to add a thin layer of a color, or want to transition from one color to another. Use a piece of sea sponge and opaque fabric paints such as those listed on page 90. Use a light touch, and gently sponge on the color. As with the other painting techniques, use a plate or flat surface as a palette, blot the sponge before applying it to fabric, and practice on scraps until you get the effect you want.

Sponging can add color, texture, and depth to your fabric.

CRAYONS

Fabric crayons can be used for iron-on colors. Try using the crayons directly on the fabric, rather than using the transfer method described on the packaging.

After drawing on the fabric with the crayon, press using either scrap fabric or white paper to set the crayon. Washfastness is NOT guaranteed. Try out the crayons on scraps of the fabric you will be drawing on, then press, to make sure there are no undesirable effects.

PERMANENT PENS (Flat Color and Metallic)

Permanent pens can be used to add details such as antennae, or for drawing decorative shapes. They are also great for outlining. Practice on a scrap of the fabric you will be drawing on to make sure that the ink doesn't spread.

Crayon was used to draw the green circles under the sprials.
Permanent pens were used for black outlines.

COLORED PENCILS

Regular colored pencils can be used for tinting and shading if the project will not be washed.

PAINTING AND DRAWING TIPS

Paint or draw on your fabric before you attach it to your project so you don't have to worry about making mistakes. Embellish a larger piece than you need so you can select the area of the embellished fabric that you like the best.

If you are uncomfortable drawing or painting free-hand, and have a light table (or makeshift light table) you can put your fabric directly over the paper pattern. You will be able to see the lines and patterns and paint or draw following the lines. (This will not work with very dark colored backgrounds.)

Use colored pencils for tinting and shading.

TYPES OF PAINTS TO USE

It's best to use paint that can be ironed. Some "puff paints" will melt and stick to your iron. If you do want to use puff paints, they must be applied as the very last step, after all fusing and ironing is done. With paints, allow them to dry thoroughly and heat set according to instructions (except puff paints). Some paints come in bottles with applicator tips that allow you to draw with the paint directly from the bottle. See Resource list on page 94 for sources of paints.

Types of paints used for the projects in this book include:

- Lumiere™ Fabric Paint
- Setacolor® Fabric Paints
- Fabric Paints by Plaid
- Jacquard® Traditional Paints
- Deka® Permanent Fabric Paints
- Versatex Textile Paints
- Neopaque™ Fabric Paint
- Acclaim Fabri-Tex is a textile medium that can be added to non-fabric water-based paints for use on fabric. It adds flexibility to dry painted surfaces and makes the paint more permanent when heat set.

If you need to paint a light color on a dark piece of fabric, use opaque paints. It also helps to paint the shape with an opaque white first, let it dry, and then paint your final color over the white.

The white areas of black and white fabric (especially geometrics) can be colored with paints, crayons, or colored pencils to create just the right touch.

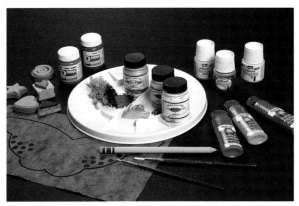

It's best to use paint that is specifically designed for fabric.

STITCHING

These quilts offer the opportunity to play with all of the decorative stitches your machine has to offer, all the way to creating your own stitches if you own an embroidery machine and the embroidery software. Experiment first on a scrap before stitching on your project. Always use a stabilizer under your stitching. This helps to prevent the "mole hills" and "tunneling" that can form while you are doing satin stitching and other heavy stitching. You can use cut-away stabilizer, tear-away stabilizer, or freezer paper. Be sure to remove the stabilizer after you complete the stitching.

Where there are multiple layers of fabric, it's often best to do the decorative stitching on individual pieces before adding them to the background layer. For example, satin stitching can be added around facial features before the entire face is fused to the background.

SATIN STITCHING

♥ If you haven't done much satin stitching, practice on some samples first—you may need to adjust your tension.

♥ Some stitchers use a lightweight bobbin thread and loosen the tension to make sure the bobbin thread doesn't show on the top. Bobbin thread is usually sold on larger spools or on pre-wound bobbins, and is most widely available in black and white. One advantage to using bobbin thread is that it doesn't add additional bulk to the back of the design.

♥ It helps to use an open-toe applique foot so you can see exactly where you're stitching.

Changing the width of your stitches adds interest.

♥ Make sure your stitch is wide enough to cover the raw edges of the fabric and that the stitch density is to your liking. Too many stitches will make the fabric pucker, causing those mole hills, while too few stitches will give an uneven look.

♥ Experiment with different stitch widths for variety. For added interest, try tapering or widening the stitches as you go—tapering to the points of leaves, or widening for decorative wedges, for example.

Pivoting

Use the needle-down position for stopping and pivoting to negotiate tight curves as well as to turn corners. The key to pivoting is to think about where you want the next stitch to be when you start stitching and leave the needle in the position that will allow you to do that.

For example, for a corner or curve, stop with the needle down on the outside edge of the stitching, lift the presser foot and turn the fabric. When you start stitching again, the needle will be on the outside edge of the new line of stitching. This allows you to stitch over the end of the previous stitching, which gives you a clean corner or curve.

When pivoting on curves, you'll get a smoother curve if you make a number of small pivots rather than just one or two.

Starting and Stopping

Starting. Make sure your starting stitches are secure. Some stitchers pull the threads to the top, knot them, them stitch over the tails for a bit, then clip. Or you can take several stitches in place, then begin.

Stopping. Pull your thread to the back, knot, and cut.

Good satin stitching takes some time and practice. Relax, put on some good music, take your time, and have fun.

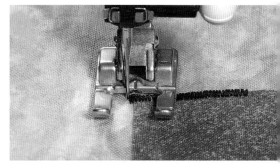

Pivoting for an outside corner or curve

Pivoting for an inside corner or curve

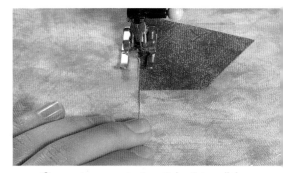

One way to secure starting stitches is to pull them to the top, knot, and stitch over the tails.

Buttonhole stitching and outlining gives a finished look.

BUTTONHOLE STITCHING

Buttonhole stitching can be used as an alternative to satin stitching. This will not give the outlined effect that lends a graphic look to most of these quilts; you may want to outline with paint or permanent pen if you choose this type of stitch.

STRAIGHT STITCHING

Details such as leaf veins, whiskers, flutter-bye antennae, etc. can be added with straight stitching. A heavier-weight cotton thread will show better than regular thread.

DECORATIVE STITCHING

If you have a machine that does embroidery stitches, this is a great opportunity to use a variety of stitches, especially geometrics—circles, triangles, wedges, or squares. If you are ambitious and have an embroidery machine and software, you can design your own stitches to use in your project.

MACHINE QUILTING

Outline quilt the major shapes or pieces to hold everything down and in place; you can use clear or colored thread. Add other decorative quilting as desired. The quilting on most of the projects in this book was kept to a minimum so as not to compete with the designs.

Straight and decorative machine stitching.

Add depth by outlining first in black, then in gold.

Combining different types of stitching adds interest.

THREADS

In addition to being a great opportunity to work with a variety of stitches, you can also play with many different types of thread. While you can use cotton thread, we recommend rayon and metallics to give you a great look on these projects. The most common threads used were 40-weight rayon and metallics.

THREAD FOR STRAIGHT STITCHING

Straight stitching can also be used to great effect, especially with a heavyweight cotton for decorative outlines and details. For quilting you can use either 100% cotton (regular or topstitch) or monofilament (nylon or polyester) thread.

THREAD FOR HAND STITCHING

Use cotton or silk thread for hand appliqué. For embellishing, you can use any type of thread you like: cotton of various weights, embroidery floss, cotton perle, metallics, and rayons.

NEEDLES

Use needles designed for the type of stitching you are doing:
- ♥ For embroidery/rayon thread use needles designed to be used with embroidery or rayon thread.
- ♥ Metallic thread: use needles designed for metallic thread.
- ♥ Nylon thread: use a needle of appropriate size for thread weight.
- ♥ Machine quilting: use a quilting or jeans needle.
- ♥ Hand quilting: use betweens, which range in size from 8 (longer) to 12 (shorter).
- ♥ Hand appliqué: use #11 Sharps or #11 Milliner's needles.

EMBELLISHING

Beads, sequins, buttons, and any other type of embellishment can be stitched on or glued.

EXPERIMENT!

Now is the time to try all of the decorative stitches your machine is capable of, or that you can program it to do. Rayon and metallic threads are perfect choices, and you can also try couching on some glorious yarns. Take a trip to your local arts and crafts store and indulge in a selection of colorful beads, or use found objects or recycled buttons. Try it all!

For sewing, use a needle and thread type that matches the type of stitching you are doing. For embellishing you can use all types of beads, buttons, and sequins.

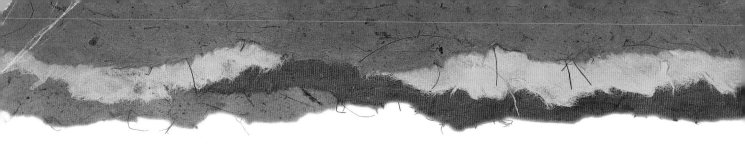

BATTING

A variety of batting was used for the different projects. A thin batting of any type is recommended: cotton, polyester, or cotton-poly blends are all fine.

NO-SEW OPTIONS

It is possible to make some of the projects in this book without sewing if the project will not be washed and or handled much. We made the *Flutter-bye Frame* (on page 24) without any sewing by painting the fabric, fusing the layers of fabric together, and cutting out the Flutter-byes and attaching them to a mat board that was then framed.

To make a project without sewing:

Follow the directions for preparing appliqué, and the Painting/Drawing instructions. It's easiest to paint the different pieces before you cut them out and fuse them together.

Rather than stitching, outline pieces with paint or permanent pen. It's best to do this before you cut out the pieces, otherwise the edges may ravel.

Cut out pieces and fuse together.

Further embellish as desired.

Paint and outline the shapes before you cut them out.

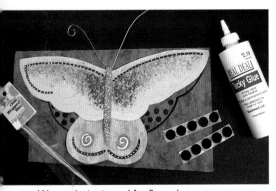

Wrapped wire is used for flutter-bye antennae.
Hook and loop dots attach the flutter-byes
to the mat board.

RESOURCES

For any art or sewing supplies check your local quilting, sewing, or art/craft stores.

For mail-order supplies try:
Cotton Patch Mail Order
3405 Hall Lane, Dept. CTB
Lafayette, Ca 94549
email: quiltusa@yahoo.com
Web: www.quiltusa.com
800-835-4418
925-283-7883

Keepsake Quilting
1-800-865-9458
Fax: 1-603-253-8346
International Orders: 1-603-253-8731

For fabric paints try:
Dharma Trading Company
800-542-5227, 415-456-7657
www.dharmatrading.com

For stamps try:
Hot Potatoes
615-269-8002
www.hotpotatoes.com

Purrfection
408-425-4743
www.purrfection.com

BIBLIOGRAPHY

Alex Andersen, *Start Quilting*, 2nd. ed., Lafayette, CA: C&T Publishing, 2001.

Harriet Hargrave, *The Art of Classic Quiltmaking*, Lafayette, CA: C&T Publishing, 2000.

Harriet Hargrave, *Mastering Machine Appliqué*, Lafayette, CA: C&T Publishing, 1991.

Jean Ray Laury, *Imagery on Fabric: A Complete Surface Design Handbook*, Lafayette, CA: C&T Publishing, 1997.

For the Laurel Burch licensed products shown throughout the book visit: **www.laurelburch.com**

OTHER FINE BOOKS FROM C&T PUBLISHING:

INDEX

For more information write for a free catalog:

C&T Publishing, Inc.
P.O. Box 1456
Lafayette, CA 94549
(800) 284-1114
e-mail: ctinfo@ctpub.com
website: www.ctpub.com

For quilting supplies:

Cotton Patch Mail Order
3405 Hall Lane, Dept. CTB
Lafayette, CA 94549
(800) 835-4418
(925) 283-7883
e-mail: quiltusa@yahoo.com
website: www.quiltusa.com

ABOUT LAUREL

Laurel Burch's Kindred Creatures are just a small part of the magical world she has enjoyed creating since she was a child living in southern California. But it wasn't until the early 1960s, after a move to the Haight-Ashbury district of San Francisco, that she began selling her hand-made jewelry in the streets and in small galleries. By the 1970s Laurel had a thriving business, and poured her passion for color and all living creatures into her art. Collectors worldwide treasure her paintings, cloisonné earrings, totebags, shirts, ceramics, resin creatures, scarves and other items for their vibrant colors and imaginative designs. The daughter of a talented seamstress, Laurel shares a special kinship with all quilters, and someday hopes to "paint" with a needle and thread.

Photo by Steve Fukuda

SHARE WITH THE WORLD FROM THE HEART OF YOUR HEART